THE SHADOW OF GOD

By Sandor Sigmond

Compiled and Edited by
Tracey Creech

LION'S PRIDE
PRESS

BEL AIR-CALIFORNIA

Layout and design by Suzie Dotan
Cover Illustration courtesy of Pat Berger
Typeface - Titles: Elysium Book, Elysium Book Italic

THE SHADOW OF GOD

By Dr. Sandor Sigmond
Author of Heal Yourself, The Book of Jade and Greenhorn

FIRST EDITION

Library of Congress Control Number: 2005927611

For information address: Lion's Pride Press, P.O. Box 491956, Barrington Post Office, Los Angeles, California 90049-9998

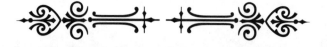

Dedicated to my grandmother, Betty,
in memoriam

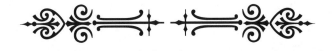

Struggle leads to victory.
Light leads to progress.

•

Can that which is unborn
Restrain its own birth into life?
Or once born—
Stay the hand of the Creator
Who is also the Master of Death.

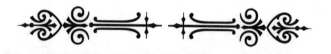

The Shadow of God

CONTENTS

Short Poems

Long Poems

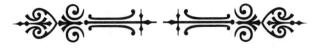

All the wisdom of man is but the accumulated knowledge of generations past. That which is written in this book has long been the heritage of the soul and the spirit of all humanity.
Humanity has always stood somewhere between the light of God and the shadow He casts upon the Earth.

Sandor Sigmond
Los Angeles, California
January 2005

INTRODUCTION

Dr. Sandor Sigmond has written thousands of poems. In his home office, where he still keeps his chiropractor's bench out to help friends in need, one finds boxes, desk drawers, and filing cabinets overflowing with notepads covered with handwritten verses, stacks of thin onion-skin pages carefully typed, and three-inch binders filled to the bursting point with computer-generated transcriptions of his life's work.

I met Sigmond six years ago when I was hired to transcribe his memoirs, which have now been published in a book called Greenhorn. Over the years I have gotten to know him, his writing and his philosophy. In this book, we have set out to present a sample of his poetry that conveys a sense of his work at large. This introduction intends to familiarize the reader with key points of his philosophy and some details of his life that may enrich the reading.

For Sigmond, a life experienced is not worth much if it is not also a life shared. His poems are a sharing of his eighty-five years of life experience; and

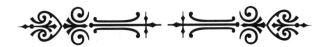

though those experiences have been extraordinary (as his memoirs reveal), the poems provide insights that everyone can understand and relate to. Indeed, Sigmond does not have much use for mysterious philosophies. The most important truths are simple, he believes, and they reside in all of us; yet we must be reminded of these truths because we so often forget them. Sigmond might see his own flashes of inspiration as his soul reminding him of something he might have forgotten-a muse of memory.

Much of Sigmond's writing draws from his personal experiences, so it is helpful to know some details. Sigmond was born on July 4, 1920, in the small Hungarian town of Bodrogkeresztur. The son of a fowl trader, young Sandor lived the life of a peasant. As a boy he was greatly influenced by his religious teacher, Rav Samuel Markowitz. Through his personal example, the rabbi ingrained in Sigmond the values of being humane even in the face of enormous adversity and of appreciating all experiences, good and bad, as essential to human development. These values gave Sigmond comfort and strength when, at the age of fourteen, he, his younger sister, and his parents were incarcerated in

Budapest as political prisoners-in part, it seems, for the crime of being Jewish. After six months in the Toloncz Ház prison, the family managed to negotiate their release. They remained in Budapest until December 1939, when the shadow of fascism and anti-Semitism that was darkening Europe convinced them to flee to America.

Reading about Sigmond's early years in Greenhorn, one is struck by his acceptance of all experiences as opportunities for growth. Sigmond remembers even the miserable conditions of Toloncz Ház as "a kind of challenge. I wondered where it would lead... I never wanted to go back to the past." While fully aware of the barbarity of his situation, he was interested in facing life's trials in a way that was both sharply realistic and meaningfully hopeful. So, as hardened inmates sobbed and his father's spirit broke, young Sigmond set about soliciting the men's stories as well as the friendship of the prison guard: "They were my teachers, this cell was my classroom, and the prison, the Toloncz Ház, was my schoolhouse." The knowledge he gained from them would help prepare him for the world outside the prison walls, not just in 1930s Budapest but for the rest

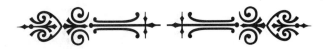

of his life. Sigmond sees experiential knowledge as the foundation for the kind of intelligent and effective action that has the power to save lives. As he says in a short poem, "Experience is a ruthless teacher, / But life needs such strength."

It is no surprise, then, that Sigmond has little patience for regret, which not only mires people in inaction but causes a more profound state of misery than painful experiences. But just because Sigmond exhorts us not to dwell in the past does not mean that he has no use for it. Quite the contrary: All of our precious knowledge comes to us from the past. The question is whether we use the past to further human progress or to retard it. "Ruthless" experiences that our ancestors have had to suffer will not be in vain if we can learn from them. History is not a dusty old book but a living, breathing teacher whose lessons we have a duty to study now.

Sigmond's meditations on failure and despair, then, are not the products of a pessimistic mind but of a hopeful one. Sigmond believes in the power of the individual to make good choices, and asks those who face seemingly hopeless situations not to abdicate this

power. In this light, we can see our struggles as primarily spiritual, and only secondarily against the outside world. Hence his concern with the health of the spirit, the true battleground of humanity.

What is the spirit, and what is God? These are questions that Sigmond anticipates in many of his short poems, yet for him they are no great mystery. In a poem that appears in his recent book Heal Yourself, Sigmond equates a person's spirit with the person himself. He describes it as "the current of life that surges continually, the light that is found in the heart and is visibly seen in the eye." God is simply the highest ideal that the human mind is capable of expressing. Key here is the word human. The human mind conceives of God and the world in human ways. It is natural to conceive of God as having human qualities, because that is how our minds work. In fact, our minds may construe God in all kinds of ways; the form is unimportant. What is important is that He is our highest ideal, and as such, we should strive to make Him manifest in ourselves and in our dealings with others as much as possible.

Though raised in Jewish tradition and learned in Jewish philosophy, Sigmond's beliefs are in fact quite

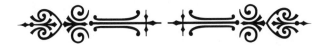

universalist. Or, perhaps it is more accurate to say that his intense meditations on Judaism have led him to find the universalism inherent within it. When asked what his religion is, he responds, "My religion is whatever God's religion is." He insists that people think deeply about what God means to them, not according to someone else's dogma. He is confident that every person can be successful in this endeavor. Thinking about God is a project that every person must take up for themselves, and in this project even the atheist has a role to play. But the existence of God is never in question. For Sigmond, God is synonymous with All Life. And who can deny All Life? To deny one's connection to All Life would be not only blind but dangerously egotistical. It is only when a person believes himself to be separate from the universe that he can believe himself to be above it, leading to tyranny; or beneath it, leading to self-annihilation.

One might read Sigmond's often didactic poems as an ongoing internal dialogue between his young, questioning human self and his ancient, all-knowing soul. But these poems are not about showcasing unique discoveries, for no discovery is truly

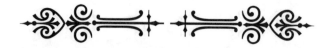

unique: "Where man builds anew / Once men before him / Did the same." Sigmond sees his work as the transmission of not only his own years of experience but of the wisdom he has received from his teachers and ancestors. Generations have a duty to share their knowledge with one another: The current generation to glean the lessons of the past, and the past generation to transmit vital knowledge to the future. How younger generations decide to interpret the actions of their ancestors is up to them, but they ignore history not only at their own peril but at the peril of all human progress. Thus humanity on a grand scale becomes a classroom of students and teachers, with each individual acting in both roles.

Sigmond sometimes employs archaisms in his poetry, such as transposed grammar, archaic words and spellings, and the like. His comfort with archaic English forms may be influenced partly by his late introduction to English (in his teenage years), and partly by his broad knowledge of old spiritual texts, whose tone he sometimes echoes. But it is also helpful to see his choice of language as seeking to supplant the primacy of the isolated self with the idea of the connected self. His use of

archaisms may be a reach back into an alternative, near-ly forgotten way of thinking that puts brotherhood before individual desire. For Sigmond, the human story is not about one person's quest for a community and his personal triumph when he finds his niche; such a view is too atomistic, assuming separate units out to encounter each other as individuals. Rather, it is about people recognizing their inherent connection to every-one and everything in the universe: people, animals, plants, oceans, stars, angels, God, their own life force. It is about recognizing humanity as a whole, and each per-son within it seeking common progress by uplifting one another. The individual is important, but he never exists simply for himself. He exists only as a part of the whole, for the benefit of the whole. The individual who seeks to separate himself from the whole has wasted his purpose for humanity, and therefore for himself.

This is why the word "I" is rare in Sigmond's poetry. When it does appear, it is most often in the phrase "I AM." Like the "light and life" of the spirit (dis-cussed earlier), we can recognize the "I AM" from Biblical texts as a signifier of God. Sigmond's insight is to personalize the "I AM" to the human being, to show

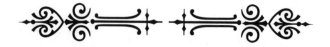

the manifestation of the divine in human life.

"I AM" is a formulation that is entirely different from the lone "I." It is the affirmation of existence. It is crucial to Sigmond because it signifies the indestructibility of the self. A person might lose everything they have, even their life, but no one can take away their "I AM." And what is at the root of this indestructible self? One's connection to the Almighty. The Almighty bequeaths existence, and once given, it can never be revoked. In this light, the self achieves the highest dignity, and hope can never be truly lost. But it is precisely because the "I AM" is given by the Almighty that one is never a lone "I." This is because the Almighty-who is synonymous with All Life-gives the "I AM" to all things. He is the original "I AM," the great "I AM." We are connected to all life through Him by virtue of this gift of "I AM." It affirms our selfhood at the same time that it connects us to everything. No one else exists that is "I," but no one can claim not to be "I AM."

A few words on form. It is probably best not to read too much into the formal mechanics of Sigmond's poems, as he is far more concerned with conveying

meaning through content and spirit. The poems in this book retain first-line capitalization, which is in keeping with his usual method; however, some archaic grammar and capitalization choices that have appeared in the poems' original versions have been modernized to make them more accessible. Sigmond is concerned that the transmission of ideas remains unfettered by mystery, and these minor amendments seek to broaden clarity and understanding.

The shorter poems in this book are often very short-sometimes only a few words long. Yet the ideas contained within them can be meditated upon for an entire day. Because many of the short poems address similar themes, they have been organized in a way that is intended to be cohesive and organic. These poems are untitled, but the themes suggested by them are listed in the table of contents in the order in which they appear.

A few of the longer poems that appear at the end of the volume have been previously published in Greenhorn: "The Ever Present Moment," "The Circle," and "Contemplation." The rest are previously unpublished, though Sigmond has delivered several of them at ceremonies.

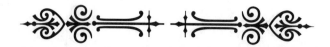

As a student of literature, as a person who is still keeping an open mind as to who or what God is, and as a member of a generation that might still be considered young, I have found Dr. Sigmond's insights to be profound, accessible, and-yes-modern. Though he speaks on occasion with an ancient voice, he reminds us that no person has ever been so old that he can afford to stop seeking answers, and no ancestor has ever been so far removed from us that his same problems and joys do not still concern us. He shows us that the old is yet new, the new is grounded in the past, and all people, alive and dead, remain connected by virtue of their eternal souls.

Dr. Sigmond's life project is to seek to understand the spirit and the soul. It is an endeavor that every generation must continue.

Tracey Creech
Los Angeles, California
January 2004

The Shadow of God

Never the apple
Without the seed.

*

Birth is the mystery,
Not death.

*

When countenance
Beholds countenance,
A universe is born.

*

Exert yourself in joy,
For in joy were you given life.

*

You must tear down before you can build.
Examine the foundation
Upon which your life stands.

*

You and your creation are one.

1

2

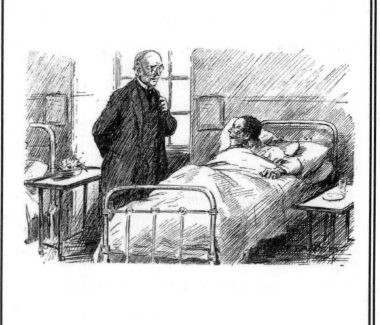

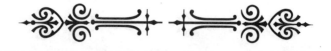

The Shadow of God

A physician can mend a wound,

But only God can heal it.

A dentist can fill a tooth,

But God must first grow it.

An architect can design,

But a workman is needed to bring it to be.

Yet, O man, you ask the architect of the universe

To design and build for you.

Where then is your own glory

In the work of Creation?

*

No one can teach

Your spirit to create-

For it created you.

*

Create not another

In your own image.

Create yourself first

Into the image
You wish yourself to be.

*

Create not a God who must obey your every wish
And whom you discard when he no longer serves
your purpose.
For a God created by man
Can never fulfill a universal plan
Nor know a universal order.

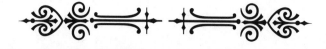

The artist
Sometimes does not recognize
His own works.

*

There is a creative spirit in you
That is perfect.
Come, know it.

*

Let your spirit expand
Beyond your body—
Beyond your mind—
Let it grow!

*

Be thankful
That you are privileged to experience
The expansion of the universe.

*

Plant a seed of trust
In the garden of the Almighty.

*

Each man is born into the world,

Yet his surroundings and his parents

Are not of his choosing.

Often they are obstacles

He needs to overcome

Before he matures

And becomes a person in his own right.

But these are also his roots

Linking him to a timeless past,

To a heritage locked within each cell in his body.

And he who makes use of his roots,

Willing to be replanted

Like a tree in new soil,

Will find his life enriched,

His heritage strengthened,

And his seed preserved forever.

*

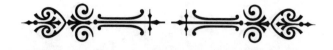

The Shadow of God

Each step,

Each stage,

Is an essential ingredient

In building the character.

Therefore accept each day

For what it is!

*

Every obstacle

Is a teacher to learn from,

Become equal to,

And finally outgrow.

*

Consider it an honor
To have many experiences and hardships
Touch your daily life.
They serve to individualize you,
To mold you into a human being

Among men who are yet to become humane.

*

I fed by the breast
Until I could grow no more.
Then I broke out, shattering my shell.
Growing in the freedom I found in myself,
I spilled the milk and ate bread instead.
I no longer seek permission to be a human being,
For my soul is not a prisoner to any man,
Nor even to me-

For my soul is me.

*

One leaf is not sufficient
To maintain the growth of a tree.

*

Green wood
Does not burn well,
Nor wet wood
Catch a spark-
*

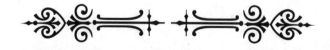

As man reaches manhood,
He begins to comprehend
His God
A little.

*

Man must accept the Earth
And make it his own,
Yet conditions on Earth
He must continue to change.

*

The purpose of life
Is always changing.
It can never be static or final–

*

As each person grows in years,
Let him also grow in maturity
And be glad that
Each year, each day, brings him
A new change.
Let the present age
Be the most happy one,
And not bygone youthful years.

*

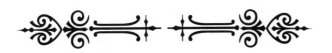

A person cannot rise so high
Before mankind, himself, or God
That he cannot fall or become disgraced.
Nor can he fall so low that
He cannot rise to the highest.
For rising and falling do not
Remain forever-
Nor does man remain on Earth forever-
*

Every return
Is preceded by a going forth.
Life precedes death.
Death precedes resurrection of the soul.
And change precedes all knowable expressions of life.
*

As the inside of a cell
Is negatively charged
And the surrounding environment
Positively charged,
Likewise is man constituted.
The character must be
Willing to receive,
And the will willing
To change.
*

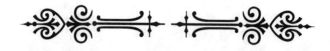

The Shadow of God

Because knowledge changes from
Growth to growth,
A man of knowledge is
Nowhere to be found.

*

God's own determination is revealed
In man's constructive actions.

*

Knowledge alone
Will never achieve
By itself.

*

Right actions save a man
From his wrong thinking.

*

Patience
Is action
Too.

*

Look for your future in actions
And not in the statements of seers.

*

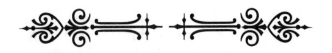

The Shadow of God

Each person
Must sooner or later
Atone for the good
That was not performed
While having the opportunity.

*

He who keeps silent
When a word must be spoken
Joins with those whose actions are against
His conscience~
Making a lie live.

*

Much energy is wasted
In making decisions
And in not making any.

*

Pride leaves he
Who boasts with lips alone.

*

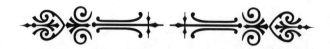

The Shadow of God

*Do not go out of your way
To seek trouble.
But when trouble
Is brought to you,
Deal with it wisely—
And never run away from it.*

*

*The ram, knowing not the
Weakness of its neck or legs,
Uses its head as a buttress
And soon learns
That the head and horns
Are not always
The means to an end.*

*

*No man
Without exposure to experience
Can know what lives beyond his own mind
Or what he may attain to.*

*

*You must experience your life
In order to know that it is God.*

*

13

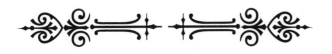

The Shadow of God

Man must experience all of his emotions
Before he can know himself.

*

It is a wise man
Who receives as his own
The wisdom gained by the experience
Of others.

*

No experience can be gained through an oracle.

*

Experience is no security against mistakes.

*

Experience is a ruthless teacher,
But life needs such strength.

*

Be not satisfied with experiences,
Or the use of people,
Or the world as a whole.
Your structures and ideals
Will offer you no refuge
From the onslaught of oblivion.

*

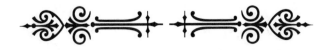

Thirst for spiritual enlightenment
Comes at any age.
It comes when one begins to wonder
What else there is besides this passing panorama,
Raising a family, attaining wealth or fame–
What else is there, besides being born into the world
And going out of it.
When these questions come upon you,
Accept their challenge.
Slowly dawn appears on your horizon,
Bringing your rebirth–
Your true birth–

*

The substance of things
That go forth to life and return from it,
Changing from one shape to another,
Display a mighty wisdom, thought and love.
O man, what this wisdom, thought and love
Write upon your person
Is knowledge you inherit from God directly.

*

Every kind of knowledge
Has its right place.
Be wise, and know
What you wish to learn.

*

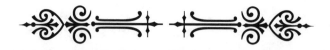

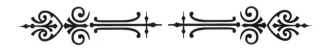

The Shadow of God

When you realize
That there is no limit
To truth, knowledge or wisdom,
You become a free man indeed.

*

Education is learning to master all situations,
Being in complete control of yourself,
And always experiencing.

*

A man's brain
May be the spirit's prison
Or its temple~
The choice is your own.

*

It is far wiser
To remove taboos
By revealing of the essence
Of taboo.

*

Should man take poison
To find out if it kills him?

*

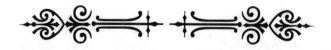

There is a time to doubt
Man or God,
Intentions and justice.
In this way man learns
To leave behind old foundations
And learns to establish new ones.

*

Wisdom above,
Doubt below~
Each complements the other.

*

Every man must doubt himself
Even to the moment of death.

*

Man creates a barrier
Between that which he does not know,
That which he ought to know,
And that which he believes he knows.
The result: static existence.

*

God is the teacher of each man from his youth.
But which man knows this,
And who recognizes his teacher?

*

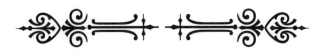

He who thinks for himself
Will seek the same right
For others.

*

Be patient with yourself
And with those around you,
For you and the world have much to learn.

*

Fear not men of great learning
Or holders of high positions,
Nor the knowledge contained in books,
Nor unjust laws.
Such men and laws are soon forgotten.
See to your own good works-
These civilization cannot forget.

*

The world
Is filled with failing men
Because they consider themselves geniuses.

*

You are one of the goals
God has set for Himself.
Now set a goal that you alone make,
And God's gifts will be yours.

*

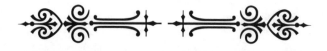

20

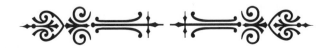

The Shadow of God

Man needs to attain many little goals
Before his ultimate objective is attained.

*

The ultimate human goal is
Complete understanding
Of the human spirit.

*

Self-confidence will do for you
What others cannot.

*

You may be able to swallow a mountain
But be blinded by a pebble.

*

There are enough obstacles to overcome
In a day's living.
Why do you seek to create more for yourself?

*

Never waste time
On the faults of human beings,
Nor on the imperfection
Of anything under the sun.
Rather use each to the benefit of all.

*

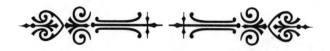

22

23

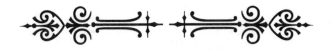

The Shadow of God

A mature person will keep faith and patience
As guideposts between which he must walk
Before he may reach his goals.

*

The highest peak cannot be reached
Without the lowest point pushing upward.

*

Challenge yourself to fail.
Maybe instead you'll succeed.

*

Sometimes it is wise to be the loser,
And much wiser to understand why.

*

Never call yourself a failure
When you try and do not succeed.
Each effort made is a stepping stone
Toward your final goal.
Be grateful that you have the opportunity to try.

*

Rather fail on your own account
Than succeed by the hand of another.

*

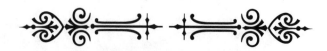

The Shadow of God

Failure is not a monster
Awaiting the opportunity
To destroy your aims, your ambition,
Your faith,
Or yourself.
It is rather an arrow
Pointing the way toward progress.

*

No man can achieve anything
That is worth something to the spirit
Without sorrow, and much travail.

*

To be able to bear a burden,
One must be worthy of it.

*

A thousand times a thousand setbacks-
This you may permit.
But defeat in your heart-
Never.

*

When failure is inevitable,
Abandon the method,
Not your goal.

*

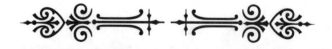

Failure is brought about by man
Believing that failing is all he deserves.

*

The prophet of failure
Is anxious to prove his prophecy.

*

Each person must come to terms
Somewhere between
His ambitions
And his limitations.

*

Failings balance man
And keep him walking on the ground.

*

A man who has not failed
Has not yet succeeded.

*

You alone define the boundaries
Of your achievements.

*

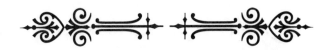

God blessed man
That he might live successfully,
But man must discover
The method.

*

When you have succeeded
In discovering a hundred or more dry wells,
You can then hope for the one
That gushes with reward.

*

Be not discouraged by failure.
The spark of life, your own,
Can never be destroyed.
You, the individual, the power to yourself,
Cannot forever die,
And no being can annihilate you
From the universe.

*

He that nurtures within himself
The I AM
Grows into oneness with the Almighty,
And~at last!~all the living
Become his personal concern.

*

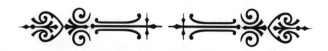

28

The I AM of your life is with you,
And no man can separate you from it.

*

Every day
You meet yourself
Face to face.

*

The diamond of your spirit
Is hidden in the clay of human nature.
Find it, grind it, cut and polish it.
Do all these for yourself—
Let none do it for you.

*

Compare not one man to another.
He is not of the same matter.
He is an individual among individuals,
A unique person to be
Discovered.

*

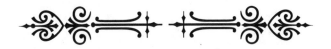

The higher entity that
Man calls the High Self,
The indestructible life
Behind the consciousness
Of everyday existence,
Is in reality himself.

*

The ability to live with yourself
Takes greater strength
Than to live with another.

*

He who gives up too easily
Abandons himself in the end.

*

Man must transcend himself
And become a part of the world.

*

Accept yourself—
For rejection has not given you much happiness
So far.

*

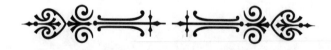

The first step to happiness
Is to accept yourself as
You are.
The next is to become relaxed
In this acceptance.
The third, to be ready to accept
The next man for what he is.
The fourth, to share yourself
With others-not to remain alone,
But to share in the joyous and sorrowful
Events of life.

*

As the sun rises
And sets of its own accord,
So let all things bring to you
Some sweetness,
Some sorrow-
For in the end, all things
Will accept you.

*

To accept one thing rather than another
Is to set aside the value of the rejected one.
Be therefore collective first,
Selective second-then will the
Values of all things become known to you.

*

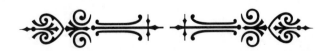

The Shadow of God

When you accept into your life
Another,
You must reflect upon the value
You will have in that person.
For with every acceptance
Comes responsibility—
And with every responsibility
Comes a higher attainment—
And with every attainment
The acceptance of a new set
Of values, endlessly growing
Without end—

*

Man must accept
In his daily living
His own inability and incapacity
To solve the problems of the world,
Or to understand
The ways of God.
Let him rather attend to the
Task at hand, and in that task
Find the meaning it has for him.

*

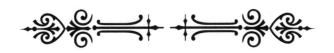

Be not like your parents,
Nor become a parent to yourself–
Be yourself!
Accept
Yourself!

*

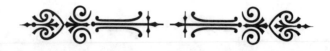

More glory is given to the Almighty
When man discovers how all things were made by Him
Than when he accepts without thought
That He made all, and is satisfied—

*

The acceptance of spiritual presence and power
Without the acceptance of the Almighty
Is as the acceptance of the tree
For the branches alone,
Without the roots and the ground
That support it.

*

Each man must exercise
His right to choose God
Or to reject Him.
Else there is no meaning for man—
Or of God for man.

*

No man makes the law of God.
No one legislates any of its particulars.
Anyone obeys or disobeys
According to the choice of his own
Conscience.

*

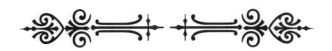

The Shadow of God

Before one obeys any law,
He must have the full right
To disobey it.

*

I must have the right
To refuse to believe
In God
And the brotherhood of the living
Before I can place trust
In Him
Or them.

*

Conscience
The consuming fire within one's soul.
Conscience
The eye that never sleeps.
Conscience
The afflicter and the healer.
Conscience
The voice of humanity.
Conscience
The master of the scales.
Conscience
The pen that writes the Book of Life.

*

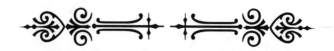

*Let your conscience be
As naked as your heart.*

*

*A clear conscience
Is man's own redeemer.*

*

*Avoid, O man,
The hell in your
Conscience.*

*

*O Man, despair not
In the face of hopeless odds.
Falter not, nor give way to fear.
Gather your strength,
And you will achieve
Whatever is meant for you to have.*

*

*Every man must have courage
If he desires to gain freedom.
Every man must have courage
If he desires to keep it.*

*

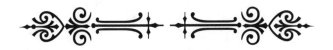

No hero is found
Where courage is wanting.
*

No grass can grow without water.
No faith can grow without courage.
*

Courage is sought
By all people.
Some find it in themselves.
Some find it through another.
Some find it only through suffering,
And many find it only in a jug of wine.
*

Man must fear more his own thoughts and feelings
Than the wrath of the unseen.
*

When fear is in you, you cry for help.
But should you be helped
When you are not willing to help yourself?
Wouldn't life mock itself by helping you
While you were unwilling
To put faith in your own soul first?
*

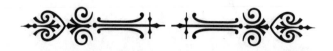

38

He who has no fear
Cannot have courage.

*

The coward is less dangerous
Than the man who has no fear.

*

Fearing one's parents
Is no sign of respect or love for them.

*

If you have love in your heart,
All your fear will vanish-
For fear and love do not abide
In the same place.

*

A tyrant or a sage
May use fear
With equal potency.

*

Fear not to grow up.
There are always new horizons
Before your heart.

*

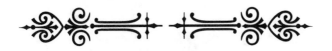

The Shadow of God

Accepting God
Out of fear
Or under duress
Is hypocrisy sublime.

*

Man need not fear the Almighty,
Though he may find reason
To fear a God,
An angel,
Or a man.

*

What ill can any man
Do to another?
Why fear any man?
The Almighty is the life of man—
Who can touch Him?
Man is imperiled by the fear
Another creates for him
And the fear that he alone accepts
And makes his own.

*

What you fear is nothing more
Than to lose your life.
But it is not to be lost.
It is always with the Almighty.

*

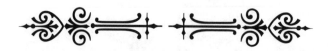

The   Shadow   of   God

41

The Shadow of God

If you know the voice
Of the spirit of the Almighty,
There will be no fear in you
When you close your eyes
And open them no more.

*

The image of fear–
The image of hell–
The image of damnation–
All are man's own creations,
Imprisoning the mind and heart.
Break them–
Cast them away–
Set yourself free–

*

Fear has no substance separate from man.

*

He who fears man, beast, or God
Fears but his own heart.

*

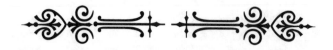

The fear you have of tomorrow
Is not a reality,
Because tomorrow does not exist.
The failures of yesterday
Are but stepping stones to a better today.
Therefore concern yourself only
With the problem at hand
Now!

*

Never be afraid to make mistakes.
They are but grinding stones to cut the rough edges
From your ways of thinking and feeling,
Enabling you to sharpen your mind
For greater achievements.

*

Do not fear your own thoughts.
Face them as you created them—
For then you can undo them.

*

Man fears the consequences of his own acts
Much more than he fears the thoughts
By which his acts were guided.

*

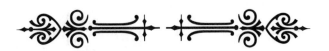

The Shadow of God

Freedom is first found
In the place where God and soul meet.
It is the heart
Wherein God speaks and the soul listens.

*

He who gives freedom to man
Gives freedom to God.
For in honoring man,
Man honors also God,
And he who restrains man
Restrains God.

*

While God gives freedom to man,
Man makes a slave of Him.

*

Release your ghosts
From the prison you have created for them.
As long as your ghosts are not free,
Neither are you.

*

Those who cry for freedom
Are often the first to deny it to others.

*

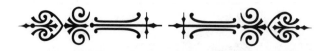

Learn to listen
And learn to respect,
For the freedom of expression
Is not limited to
The exclusive right
Of one or a few.
*

Duty and loyalty must also offer
Freedom from them
If life is to have any meaning.
*

A man seeks freedom,
Yet enslaves himself
In mind and body
For an ideal he seldom understands.
*

Fear not to lose your freedom,
For a free man never claims to possess it–
He gives it to others.
*

Destiny rules he who has abandoned freedom.
*

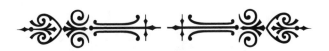

A servant is made to believe
That he needs the master to do his thinking.
The master views his servant as an eternal child,
Needing his constant care,
While unknown to him the servant builds
His resentment, plans destruction,
And rejoices in his master's downfall.
Set not yourself up as a master over
Anyone, that you may not reap
An unwanted harvest.

*

He who rules another by force
Is a servant and a tyrant in the same instant.

*

Seek freedom
From oppressors of the heart and spirit,
But do not seek to be free
From the responsibilities of life.

*

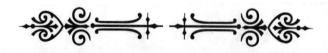

Man seeks freedom
To choose among religions
That are but creations of men,
But the Giver of Life
Gave no religion to anyone.
A way of life
Is for each to discover
In one's own life
Every day.

*

Freedom is a word
Dying in meaning.
Unless man decides to rescue it
And restore it in his own
And in his fellow man's life,
Slavery will take its place.

*

An unwilling captive,
Be it beast or man,
Can never be a friend.

*

He who seeks freedom
For the soul alone
Seeks but half of the man.

*

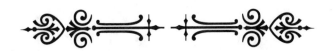

Freedom is found everywhere,
Even in the midst of enslavement.

*

He who is tied down to another
Is never free
To give of himself to anyone.

*

To become a free person,
The struggle must come from
Within.

*

Be a master if you will,
But have no man as your servant.
Be a servant if you will,
But have no man as your master.

*

You may hear many fables
Of the enslaved man and the free-
But remember,
They are all about you.

*

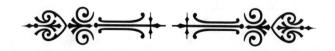

Enslave not your fellow man
By act or thought,
For in the end
He free
And you slave
Shall be wrought.

*

No man can be held
As a slave in his heart
Unless he accepts his slavery.

*

One man has the right to dispute
Another man's truth.
One man may doubt
Another man's intentions.
But no man can dispute
Another man's acceptance
Of that which is beautiful and
Pleasing to him alone.

*

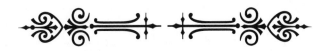

The Shadow of God

Look in the eyes of children
And you will see unmarred beauty.
Look in the eyes of lovers
And see beauty as it is seen by them.
Look in the eyes of he who has faith in man
And you will behold that beauty that is
The salvation of mankind.

*

Within each living being
There is as much ugliness as beauty,
As much goodness as wickedness,
As much hate as love,
As much wisdom as ignorance.
No one is free of these
If one is a living being.
The elements alone are free from these.
Let no one credit himself for being alive!
One inherits his life
From the fount of all the living-
The Supreme All Life!

*

To desire something too much
Makes attaining it impossible.

*

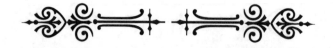

The beginning of all human achievement
Lies in a desire.

*

Desire to achieve
That which you are afraid of,
Because you may fail.

*

Teach yourself to desire,
But first desire knowledge.

*

Be silent in your conduct.
Speak but few words.
Carry your load well.
Desire but minimum in all things.

*

Love yourself sufficiently
To forgive yourself.
In doing this,
You will be loved by others
And forgiven by them.

*

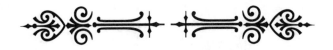

Never condemn anyone.
It is enough that he condemns himself
For things he alone knows–
Forgive him!
For he too has problems that
Make him afraid to live.

*

To condemn,
One needs little wisdom.
To forgive,
One needs more than wisdom.

*

Why should one person
Forgive another?
You may ask–
How fair, how honest
In feelings, thought and action
Are you
All the time?

*

When you forgive,
You must also forget–
But can you do it?
The Almighty alone
Is capable of it!

*

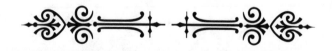

Release your God
And your guardians
From the heavy vows
You have placed upon them,
For not all vows
May be carried out.

*

Many wrongful acts are committed against God
By failure to revoke a prayer
Made without thought
Of the prayer's consequences.

*

Repentance and forgiveness
Cannot be expressed
In words alone.

*

Often it is necessary to repent and forgive
Long after the guilty one has left the world.

*

He who defames another
Will in the end be defamed.
But he who defames his ancestors
Will require the forgiveness of all.

*

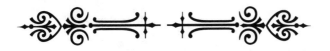

He who forgives
Uses the key
To a new day~
A new year~
A new life!

*

To receive forgiveness without true repentance
Is to steal from the forgiver's heart.

*

Forgiveness and understanding are inseparable.

*

Drift not, O soul, from place to place.
Feel not anger toward the living.
Forgive us for our ignorance,
For not thanking you for your sacrifices,
For not appreciating your deeds.
As mortals we do not think too clearly.
You, O soul,
May now rest your weary self.
But return to inspire us
To build a better world
Wherein your hopes and labors
Will add to the glory of humanity
Before the rays of the Almighty's light.

*

It is not God who gives a slice of bread to the hungry,
Nor He who sews cloth into garments.
It is man who does these things
For himself and others.
But it is God who gives us wheat for bread,
Material for raiment,
And the intelligence to know how to make use of them.

*

God is the giver of life.
You are its distributor!
Should the distributor lack in supply?

*

The gift that the Almighty
Gave to you to use
Must be used for all His children
And all His creatures,
Or else it will work against you—
For the power of the spirit
Cannot be choked off.
It must be expressed!

*

God never gives—
Nor does He withhold—
Nor does He take anything away—

*

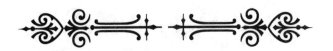

The Shadow of God

There are no final gifts from anyone,
Not even from God~
And there are no final solutions
To any problems.

*

Immortality is not a gift
But an inherent quality of life itself.

*

An other is simply your left hand
To whom your right is giving;
So whatever you give to another,
You give to yourself.

*

What can man give to God?
Food? He needs it not.
Clothing? He needs it not.
But give these things to man.
And you will have given to God.

*

He who believes
That he is God's favorite
Is already in darkness.

*

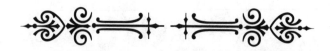

In the brotherhood of life,
None stands in rank above another.
He who separates himself from this common bond
Separates man from man,
And darkness is his master.

*

Whatever darkness
Exists amongst men
Has started by men
And must come to an end
By men.

*

Evil is a good teacher.
Good is a better one.

*

It is wrong to forget what is evil in man—
And it is wrong to forget what is good in him.

*

Accept the evil that exists inside you—
And that which is good.
Accept the good and the evil
That exist outside of you—
For between these
Lies the narrow road of your life.

*

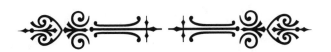

The Shadow of God

The belief in evil
Captures the imagination more rapidly
Than the belief in good.

*

God cannot destroy evil–
For it is man's creation.

*

The name of the devil is self–
The self of every man.
His home–man.
His emissary–man.

*

The inharmonious blending
Of that which is good
Creates evil.

*

There are those who see evil
Around everyone they meet,
And at the same time believe
They are above it,
And pray to God
Requesting the destruction of men
Who oppose their views–
Are you one of these?

*

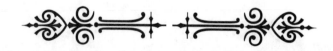

The future belongs to that generation
That recognizes the evil and the good in itself,
And understands that one grows
At the expense of the other.

*

Houses may decay,
Flesh may rot,
The sword may turn to rust—
But evil endures
In the ways of men.

*

It is easy to overlook and in time to forget
The torture that one man does to another
As long as it is not done to himself.

*

A snap on the rein
Is more painful for the horse
Than a hundred lashes on its back.

*

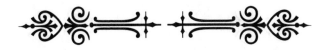

The Shadow of God

The most unhappy people
Fill their hearts and minds
With the belief that there is
Reward for such misery.
So they refuse to change their hearts
And reject what the moment brings
Before their eyes to behold and
Into their hands to grasp.

*

Most everyone
Destroys himself
Without a cause.

*

He who endures suffering
Without determining its cause
Deserves to suffer.
He who endures the evil
Directed against him or those he loves
Encourages evil, and deserves it,
For he is no better
Than the cause.

*

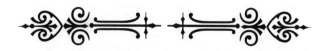

Man suffers
Because he believes
That God is ready to punish him
For any small wrong
He may commit.
He makes of God
A Peeping Tom,
A lowdown spy.
It is this belief that binds him
To the darkness of his condition.

*

God does not punish any man.
It is enough that man does it to himself.

*

Man punishes himself.
No one else can do it for him
More and better.

*

Outward happiness is no substitute for inner misery.

*

Without disappointment or grief
To gnaw at the heart,
No room can be carved
To hold joy within it.

*

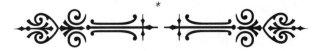

62

The cave may be damp,
But it gives some warmth-

*

A single act of anger
Stops many a good thing
From ever coming to you.

*

Shepherd, be not angry.
You will blind the leading ram,
He will stumble,
And with him will go the flock.

*

Between man and a God
Deception is always possible.
Between man and Life
No deception can wedge itself.

*

The utterances of deceiving tongues
Have oft uprooted a well-treed forest.

*

The only person that man ever fooled was himself.

*

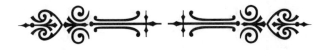

63

A lying tongue becomes loathsome
Even to those who delight in listening to it.

*

Rather be wounded
By your friend
Than with a deceitful heart
Embraced by your enemy.

*

To deceive others
Is to willfully deceive yourself.

*

Lies are like a field of roses.
One dares not walk among them
Lest the thorns wound his flesh or rend his garment.
He admires them from a distance.

*

When the Earth is no more,
And the stars become like dust,
And the solar systems become like swamps
In the midst of the Milky Way,
The Almighty will still be where
The Earth and stars were laboring
Among the elements.

*

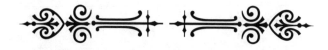

Everything men hold onto
As something of value
Have they borrowed for a time
From the earth.

*

Gold and silver-
Bricks of mortar-
Edifices great or small-
Statues and sailing ships-
Iron and copper-
Oil and bread-
All come from that upon which
Man sheds his blood,
In war or peace-
It's always the same-
The one and only
Earth.

*

Those who believe the Earth
Lacks God's presence
Will never find any use
For anything
In any world-

*

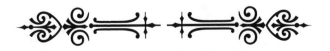

Break the barrier
Between your awareness of the day
And the soul that beats near your heart
To the tune of life–
Your own–your own–

*

In the light of the sun of spirit,
Begin your day's work.
Seek shelter under the wings of the Almighty
As your night approaches.

*

Each day recreates itself
From its yesterdays.

*

Whose day is lived right,
His tomorrow is already bright.

*

In the course of a day
Many are joyous,
Many are tearful,
Many are born to life,
Many are born through death.
In this very day,
The future is linked with its past.

*

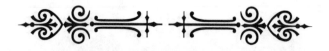

The Shadow of God

The alpha and omega of all men
Is a day.

*

Eternity is but one day.

*

A man's day must count for something,
Or else his days will be counted.

*

A day is heaven
For some.
A day may be hell
For others.
A day may be a door,
A garden,
Or a desolate road.
A day is something for everyone.
But a day has no meaning
Without a someone–
Without a you.

*

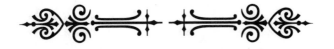

In a day the earth
Can change its shape and form.
In a day nations
Can be destroyed or reborn.
In a day, millions
May die of disease and hunger.
Or, in a day, life
Can renew itself.
In a day
Life begins
And life ends-

*

The body is the mirror of character.

*

Man cannot benefit from his body
Unless he maintains its good health.
Man cannot gain the benefits of his mind
Unless he uses it.
Man cannot know life
Unless he goes out to meet it.
Man cannot know God or what He can do
Unless man recognizes and makes use of Him.

*

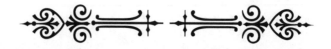

The feet of man
Have danced in joy
And marched to war,
Have trampled in mud
Of the tiller's field,
Have followed solemnly
In mournful procession,
Have jumped up and down
Upon counters and ladders,
Have marched in protest
For some cause--
All the while they trod
Upon the highway of hope,
And shall do so until man learns to walk with his
soul.

*

God's feet have oft trembled
Under the weight of man's responsibilities.

*

As blood is carried from the heart
Throughout the body,
So does God vivify man,
His life flowing through his soul.

*

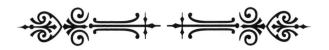

The head can but think;
The heart, but pump blood;
The feet, but walk or dance;
The hand, but hold, caress or work.
Ask of God only that which He can do,
And not that which you can do for yourself.

*

Courtesy comforts
Like a fresh drink upon a dry lip
Or fine oil upon a tired body.

*

It is better to go hungry
Than to burden the body
With foods that poison it.

*

God speaks not
With the voice of man,
Yet in man's voice
God's own soul
Can be found.

*

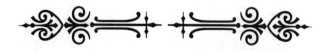

Air in motion
Striking the eardrum
Is not the only sound
That can be heard,
For the movement of lips is
Not the only way to speak~

*

The unspoken gratitude of the heart
Means more than hollow words of the mouth.

*

The face of God
Is found in man~
Some sad~others smiling~
Foreheads wrinkled~with weather~beaten eyes~
Some girt in angry lines~
While others reveal a gentle love.
Behold, O man, how you regard your fellow.

*

The eyes of man are on his face,
Directed away from himself.
They can never see his own back,
Where God stands to guide him.

*

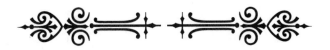

The   Shadow   of   God

What is that light we call God?
Is it what your eyes can see,
Like sunshine
Or stars in the night's darkness?
Is it conscience?
Or the potential of your being?
No, none of these,
For these are results.
God's light is yourself.
He lives in your highest consciousness,
Never erring,
Always knowing, always expanding
The man that is you.

*

Man forever needs to represent God in an image
So that God can be intelligible to his senses;
But happy is the man whose images
Cease to haunt his mind by day
Or his nightly dreams.

*

Man's God is bound by his own conceptions.
The wider and higher his spiritual vision,
The mightier his God will be.

*

Man's vanity caused him to pretend
That God is like himself in shape and form,
Intellect and reason-
Thus man's God is but a shadow of himself.
O man, stop creating gods
And projecting them upon clouds on high,
For the true God is not an extension of yourself,
Nor is He one of your faculties.

*

The eye of man
Is the image
Of man as a principle.

*

Aspire not toward the heaven
You cannot see.

*

Man's eyes may not see you,
But the eye of your life constantly observes.

*

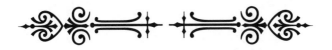

The Shadow of God

He who sees in God only that which is good
Sees with the eyes of men
Which see only what they want to see in Him.

He who sees in God
Good as well as bad
Sees Him better,
Yet still with eyes of men.

He who sees in God
Good as the ripeness
And bad as the immaturity
Of understanding
Sees clearly.

*

Do not attend to your appearance alone,
For you may become
A mausoleum—
Beautiful to eyes,
But a carcass within.

*

A duck, while its head is down,
Keeps its eyes looking into the distance.
Follow its example.

*

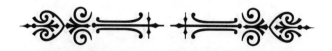

74

The eye of God
Beholds the desires of men,
But the eyes of men
See not the presence
Even of their own life~

*

See the world moving around you.
Be fascinated by the lives of others.
Forget yourself~
Marvel at the world~

*

Stare not into the sun
In hopes of finding out its secrets.
Your eyes will lose their power
And the secrets beneath your feet
Will be lost forever.

*

Man often sees a vision of himself
In which he feels the pain or joy
He has done to others,
Believing that it's someone else
Doing it to him~

*

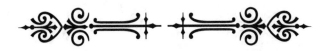

Dreams are old grapes
In new presses–
Their meaning, aged wine
In different bottles.

*

In a bed
Many are born.
If fortunate,
In bed one may die.
In bed
Some may laugh
Or love,
And some may weep
And cry.
The bed:
Friend to the sick,
Enemy to those crippled
In body or mind.
The bed will remain
Friend or foe
Depending on each one's
Blessings or woes.

*

No bed can carry
Anyone's burden,
Nor blankets comfort
The unloved.

*

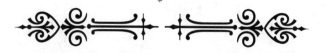

The robes of a saint
Do not necessarily cover a saint.
*

Others may design and manufacture
What each body desires to wear.
But man's spirit must wear
His own fashions.
*

To the babe in the crib,
The mother is its goddess.
She nurtures and comforts him.
The father is its god.
In his arm, the babe feels
Strength and security.
The physician or midwife
First delivered it into life.
Beware what you do with these images
Later in your life.
*

When a child learns to walk,
He also learns to fall.
*

Children are bound
To be wiser than their parents
And their teachers
In many respects.
*

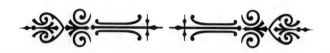

No teacher should resent
Children with greater
Capacity for life
Than themselves,
But rather be glad
To guide them
Rightly
Along their life's
True path.

*

A child who is a rebel
Has a cause for being one.

*

Children need special
Understanding.
And he who has the wisdom
To understand a child
Will never grow old.

*

Children need to be wiser
Than their parents,
For in their wisdom
Is their future contained.

*

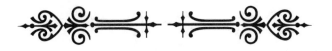

When a child is happy,
The sun fires forth
A ray-
*

The child keeps
The memory of his parents
Green in his heart,
Whatever those
Memories be.
*

A child has true compassion.
Teach yourself to follow.
*

The smallest child may be the wisest sage.
*

Children's prayers
In their simple words
Are always heard first.
*

A helpless child
Has often saved
A helpful man.
*

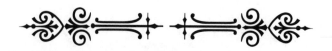

*The tears of a child
Are the rivers of new
Creation.*

*

*Yesteryear we were
The children of
Someone's tomorrow.
The morrow has come-
And we are it.
Behold the vanishing hope of
Yesteryear.*

*

*Children grow to be your equal.
But equality is not good enough.
They should outgrow you,
And you must become their past.*

*

*Give the child of today
A chance to grow,
To set up his own rules.
To think for him,
To lay down laws for him,
Is to recreate
The child in our image
And force upon him the
Habit of not thinking.*

*

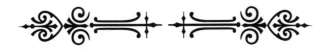

Children look to you
For guidance.
Children look to you
For support and strength.
Be considerate toward them.
They are little people
With feelings, with problems.
Help them by discovering
Them-and in them
Something good of yourself.
*

It is a strain
On a young child's body
To contain the presence
Of the Almighty's spirit.
Be therefore gentle toward
Your child,
That such a burden
May not be frightful to him.
*

All a parent can do
Is provide the best environment for his child
In which to grow to maturity.
As every plant needs certain soil
And certain shade in which to grow,
So do children born in the same household.
Parents, look to how you raise your own seed.
*

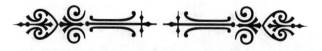

The Shadow of God

From the issue of
A foolish man,
A wise one may be born;
From the issue of a
Wise man,
A fool to plague him.
*

Affection is often used
As a snare to trap a child
And force him into obedience.
*

Do not smother
The curiosity of your child.
Do not break his
Soul, his individuality,
To recreate
The monstrosity
You find in yourself
Which was perpetuated
By your ancestors
Before you–
*

Children do all things
For the parent of the opposite sex,
And learn all things from
The parent of the same sex.
*

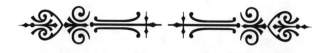

The Shadow of God

Loveless children

Establish loveless homes—

Loveless homes are torn homes—

Torn homes, torn countries—

Torn countries, torn civilization—

What future is there in this?

*

Without trials, without sorrow,

Without difficulties to overcome,

Man begins to decay

Regardless of his age in years.

*

No one wishes to lose the illusions of youth,

Nor accept the advance of years.

*

Old age atones

For youthful mistakes.

*

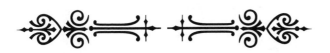

Behold, O old man~
Your arched back of today,
Your wobbly feet
And trembling hand.
The troubles of your years weigh you down.
Yet not so long ago
You were but a babe, a suckling
In someone's arms.
What has happened to you, O old man,
With your future now behind you~
Where is your hope?
Your hoary head~
Many tales it could tell
Of loves, of dreams,
Of hopes and purposes.
Yet O~old man~you are blessed,
For not every youth has a chance
Of ever becoming a man~old~like you.
*

In youthful eyes
An aged soul
Is oft found;
But sometimes
In an aged face
No soul is to be found.
*

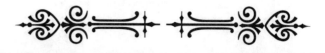

To attain old age is good.
To attain old age and wisdom is better still.
But to be aged and loved
Is the crowning glory
Of a life that has been lived.

*

An aged soul is beloved by God.

*

Bow not to anyone
Because of his age.
Rather bow to the wisdom
That comes forth from him.

*

Reassurance that an aged one
Is still useful to someone,
Or to himself,
Is all that he seeks.

*

Age is an affliction of the past,
The endowment of the previous generation.
The present generation seeks to bring into the future
All of its misconceptions and errors.
Woe to all of us
That we still see in ignorance some bliss!

*

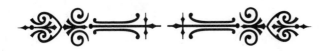

To know that one has lived even a day
Is to feel sure that one is a person,
A being with a past,
Belonging to the history of the world.
*

Where man builds anew
Once men before him
Did the same.
*

Your ancestors are
What you will be,
And you are
As your ancestors were.
Therefore be considerate
In your dealings
With either generation—
The ones who are leaving,
The ones who are gone,
The ones who are growing,
The ones yet to be born—
For you contribute
To the well being of all.
*

Whatever one generation forgets,
Future ones must remember.
*

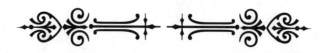

Humanity is surrounded with
The thoughts of bygone generations
That still hold sway over
The present.

*

Each person sooner or later
Rebels
Against the laws of the land he lives in,
The society in which he dwells,
Or humanity's slow progress.

*

Were man to write the history
Of the Almighty's achievements on Earth
And compare it with that of man,
Man would have to hide his face in shame
Before all the living-
Seeing the opportunities he was given but that he missed,
The aid he was offered but that he refused,
The guidance available but that he cast aside,
The friendship extended but that he shut out.
It is right that this shame
Be upon the face of man!

*

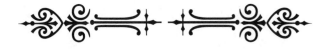

For the sake of freedom
Or the sake of tyranny,
Women become widows,
Children fatherless.
The earth is torn and
Soaked with blood,
Opening its mouth
To swallow lifeless forms,
Only to be forgotten
As time wipes memories away
In a shameless age,
A page in an unworthy human history.
*

Each civilization builds itself up
And then hastens to destroy itself.
This is the sum of all civilizations
That have no regard for the humane
Or for the truth of God in all.
*

As the planets must follow the sun
In their journey through the stars,
So each generation must follow another.
As planets cannot take the place of the sun,
So no generation can take the place of the preceding one.
*

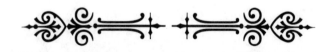

The Shadow of God

He who lays claim to a legacy
Must be willing to bear its burden,
Be it honor or dishonor,
Pride or shame.

*

One generation cannot judge another,
For each generation manifests
The strengths and weaknesses
Of its predecessors,
And all generations atone for the mistakes of another.

*

To look into the past
With remorse
And regret
Is to waste the opportunities
Of the present
And rob oneself of
The time needed to
Handle the problems at
Hand.

*

Most practical men
Are slaves to a politician
Or a half-wit economist.

*

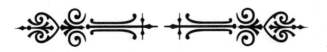

More politicians lead their nations to ruin
Than the bombs of the enemy.
From the enemy, there is some defense.
But who can defend himself
From the tongue of a politician?

*

Accuse not the Almighty
For the acts of a man or a nation.

*

Let no one belittle the little man~
For as small grass is the food of cattle
And tall grass the hiding place of lions,
So is the little man the support of a nation
And the boastful man the breeder of trouble.

*

Death~
What is it?
A door~a hallway?
A person? A beast that stands in ambush
To devour its prey?
No~
Death is but a condition
Without substance, without form.
And there is no death to life~
Only to form.

*

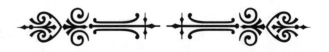

What is the hereafter,
To whom does it belong,
And who goes there?
Contemplate it with your heart,
And see that hereafter is now.
Then you'll need not be surprised or perplexed
When you meet it.

*

The netherworld of man is in his mind.
It creates distress in waking hours
And sorrow at nightfall.
And death follows each dream.
But man must learn to overcome them
Ere he awakes.

*

Man creates the image of death
Within his mind,
But it is with his hands
That he destroys himself.

*

The man who walks with truth
Will not fall victim to death,
Nor will tears roll on his cheek
Or be wasted in the wind,
For deliverance is with him
From the beginning.

*

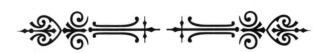

Seek not death.
Seek forever life.
Express it.
Hear its voice.
*

The power by which
You long to die
Is the same power
By which you came
To life.
*

Death rips away the mask,
And the soul reveals his nakedness
For all to behold.
*

As rivers dry up and waters disappear,
So is the mortal man.
In time he lies down and wakes
Not up again.
*

A man goes down into death
Like water that seeps into the soil,
Whence it cannot be gathered forever.
*

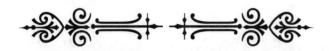

Souls are not banished forever
From beholding the face of God.
But many a soul is banished
From beholding the face
Of the person he loves.

*

The so-called dead
Do not leave you!

*

Many women are killed each day
By giving birth to children
Conceived without love.

*

True death comes to a man
When he refuses to acknowledge
The life that is in all.

*

Many a death is caused
By the slow suffocation
Of boredom.

*

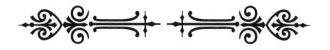

Life can never be shut up
Or imprisoned by the grave.
*

Death touches not
That which lives~
Only that which is dead already.
*

Death walks by you
Each and every day.
But so does God~
And your life~
*

Man in his private thoughts
Often converses with death
And confesses to him
His most secret feelings.
*

The mourners know not
What they mourn,
For they believe the flesh
To be the man
And see not the life
That is now with
The Almighty.
*

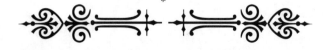

In dying,
One does not redeem himself–

*

Death cannot release the soul
From its responsibilities,
Nor can it bring peace.

*

Wait not 'til the hour of death
To improve, or to live–
For real life is you today,
And death will not reward you
For work not achieved–

*

Cause not the silver cord to snap
Nor the golden bowl to break
By your hand or testimony.

*

The consequence of death is always life.
The seed dies; from it a bloom comes forth.
A silkworm dies, and a butterfly emerges.

*

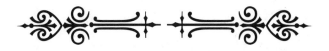

The great secret of living lies in alternating
Between the momentary problem and inner reality,
Between the ridiculous and sublime,
Between dejection and hope,
Between man and God,
Between reason and faith—
Between all that oppose each other.

*

That which separated
Man from God
Is man's concept
Of unity.

*

The light of each day
Is incomplete
Without the darkness
Of the night—

*

Because of the dark side in man,
The light of reflection is able to develop.

*

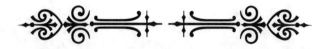

The Shadow of God

As fire rages upward
And water flows downward,
So does a man
Torn between right and wrong.

*

Each man in his life must perform
At least one good deed
And one misdeed.

*

For some the power of God
Cannot be real
Without the contrasting image
Of the devil.

*

Life interweaves and relates.
Human nature
Differentiates,
Clarifies,
Discriminates,
And remains
Detached
In all things.

*

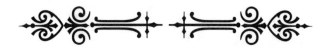

The Shadow of God

Where is the dignity of man
When he must accept a god
Out of fear
That he will be thrown to lions,
Or be given to Satan to be tormented eternally,
Or will not resurrect if he does not accept a creed-
Or suffer guilt and remorse for his conduct?
I want a God who will accept me in my shortcom-
ings and failures,
Who will complete me where I need to be completed,
Who will help me where I cannot help myself,
Who will teach me where I lack in knowledge or
common sense,
Who will make me carry my burden when it is mine
to carry,
Who will not let me transfer my responsibility to
Him or some other person when it is my own.
I want a God who can refuse my prayers and
desires.
I want a God to whom I can speak any way I
choose.
My God must be beyond my reach forever,

100

But close enough so that we can both communicate,
If we both so desire,
Without anyone else between us.

*

Man is a person.
God is the All Person.
It is natural that two persons
Should have a dialogue
And share the secrets
Of their innermost hearts.

*

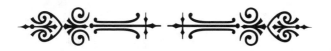

God speaks to every heart
A syllable at a time each day.
A ray of his love shines
And lights up the caverns of the mind.
His grace flows one drop at a time,
Like dew refreshing the soul
At the dawn of labor.

*

Within each being
The divine consciousness must grow,
Or else the spirit remains damp and dark,
And the character
And the individual
Remain incomplete-

*

He who runs after God
Will not find Him,
For in running too hard
His eyes do not see
That God is running behind him
Glued to his back
Closer than the skin around his flesh-

*

This is your birthright, O man:
Because you are alive,
You are life.
Because you are life,
You are spirit.
Because you are a spirit,
You will live in eternity.
This is your heritage
Endowed by the supreme spirit,
The Almighty.

*

Prayer without love is worthless.

*

The Almighty must express Himself
In the soul of each,
And each soul
Must become expressed in Him.

*

Polish the diamond in the rough
That it may become the jewel of your soul
And your God within may become manifest.

*

The foundation of foundation
Is the Almighty.

*

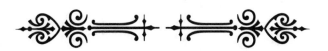

Seek not for God outside of you
But within all beings-
Including you.

*

A godless age is as much of a blessing
As an age filled with gods.
One burdens the mind with doctrines;
The other cleans it
And forces it to mature.

*

Call upon the Almighty
Day by day.
Form words in your heart.
Speak the language
Of your own creation and invention.
Follow your own light.
And in your distress,
He will surely answer you,
And you will be pleased.

*

The universe is the temple of every man,
The grand mansion of the spirit sun
That reflects the presence
Of Almighty God
In the human soul.

*

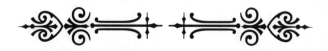

Each man has a name,
And man names all that he sees.
God is a name, a rank, a symbol
To a spirit.
Man thus can comprehend God,
For God is a man–
Compassionate, forgiving, or jealous–
Like a man.
But the blessed Almighty remains
The nameless Life,
The nameless Light–
Though having many names.
He stands firm and hidden in the cosmos
Which is a mask, an expression–
His shadow–
Forever enduring
In timeless change–

*

The Almighty does
What He wills
And when it pleases Him.
Do not be too curious
About His plans for you
Or for anyone else.

*

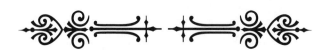

Know!
That your life
Is a spark of the Almighty
Dwelling in you.
Find it,
Know it,
Be guided by it,
Love it,
And in turn you will love the It
In all beings,
Both seen and unseen.

*

O Thou Supreme One Spirit Great,
Hear the words in my heart,
My supplication and my cry.
You are my life—
The star—the sun of my being—
The friend who never tires—
The teacher who never admonishes, but only
suggests—
The father who always provides—
The mother who gives precious gifts—
The Ever Present One.
When your host, like men,

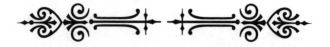

The Shadow of God

Become impatient and leave,
And all companionship is gone,
Thou, O Supreme One Spirit Great,
Remain faithful, through all time,
The true friend forever.
You are my very life, the life of me,
And my ever present light!

*

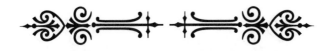

The Shadow of God

Why does my Soul,
O Almighty,
Search for the peace
That rests with you alone?
*

When the fury of great winds
Still the faint voice,
When thundering storms
Blot out a cry,
O God‒
Be with me‒
Leave me not alone‒
*

In the imaginable beginnings,
The universe was but
The One Spirit,
The One Soul,
The One Mind.
The Almighty was the All.
He was the Time.
He was the Space.
He was the Motion.
He was the Essence, and Substance
Of the All.
The All
Of the All
Was He.
*

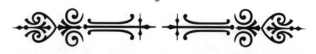

He who cannot find the Almighty
Outside of himself
Will not find Him
Inside of himself.
*

Contact the Almighty each day
And release Him from the obligation
That you placed upon Him yesterday,
For yesterday's request
May not be worthy of an answer.
*

A prayer to the Almighty
Is man's key
To enter His chambers
And plead his cause,
Whatever it be.
*

One cannot plant corn
Where corn is absent.
One cannot evoke wisdom
Where wisdom was never stored.
One cannot evoke love
When one was not loved.
One cannot find truth
When truth was never known.
One cannot invoke God
Where God does not exist.
*

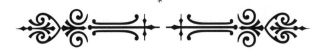

He who asks
What Does God Require Of Me
Turns God into a dictator.
This act will quench his vitality
And void his reason for living.
It removes his right to make decisions.
But when he asks
What Does God Mean To Me
He uses the accumulated
Wisdom of humanity and God
To enrich himself.
He acts to become a free person,
A true individual among individuals.

*

Have you ever found a man
As holy as God,
Or as complete as God's universe?
If your answer is in the positive,
You are a slave to an illusion;
And if it be in the negative,
You are in need of much learning.

*

He who seeks God and faith
Must seek it in humanity
As well as in himself.

*

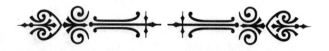

The Shadow of God

God is not found outside of matter.
He is the active, potent life within it.
He has never abandoned that
Which He brought into existence.

*

A promising God,
Like a promising man,
Is not to be trusted.

*

The gods of the past are buried with those who
created them.
The gods created now will also be buried with those
who create them.
But the All Life—
Who can create Him—
Who can bury Him?

*

The Creator gave equal opportunity to each
To advance in soul,
Yet not every person has equal opportunity
To care for his needs in the flesh.

*

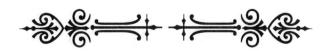

The Shadow of God

Take a flower in your hand,
Or a pebble, or a grain of sand.
Examine it
And you'll discover God's ways
For yourself.

*

Accept not another man's image of a God
As your own,
For it will not bring you any happiness.
But try to discover the meaning
Of your God, in your life,
Every time you can spare the thought.

*

God heals slowly.

*

Release God and your guardian angels
From responsibility to you.
Then you will mature in soul
Instead of being a burden,
And become a coworker
In this world of yours.

*

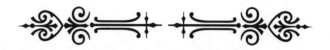

God is life,
And He cannot take it away
Without destroying a part of Himself.

*

If God be dead–
Good!
For now the image
Has fallen–
And God
In the form of progress
Can manifest in your life–

*

The vainest of men
Will distrust he who constantly praises him
Or lauds him
Or lures him with gifts.
Can you hope to sway God
With your flattery,
With your gifts?
Should He not distrust you?

*

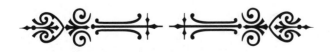

Thou O God—
Thou O Life—
Thou O Man—
Are always known
And revealed,
For nothing exists
That isolates Thee
From the I
Of being—

*

The God of another
Will not serve your needs more
Than the God you abandoned
For reasons of your own.

*

God is not where man believes he is,
But where man finds Him
Every moment of his days.

*

God alone is the wealth
Every man should strive for.

*

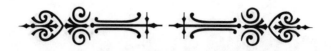

Blessed is the man who never discovers God
In the fullness of His being
But finds Him daily working by his side.

*

He who has no confidence in his God
Cannot have confidence in himself.

*

Though mind be gone,
Spirit still rules.
When spirit be gone,
God rules.

*

God granted to each being
A right to live and be happy—
Therefore grant it to yourself
And to your fellow man.

*

God as a powerful impulse of the soul is the
God we must be concerned with.
For God as an impulse can be affected—
We can affect it.
This God is the knowable one.

*

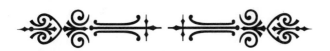

Nothing is acceptable to God through proxies.
Each man himself must appear before Him,
Unafraid.

*

Man must give authority to God
So that He may be able to do something for him.
But authority must not be given too late,
Or as an alternate measure.

*

As you raise others,
So does He raise you,
So does He bless you.

*

He who looks for God
In a far-off place
Will never find Him.
But he who looks for Him
In his very self
Will experience Him.

*

God's spirit is that
Which God has become
To man.

*

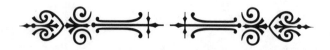

What God is
Is up to man.
What God can do
Is what man lets Him do.

*

God and man share the same universe.

*

God the master-
Life the mistress-
Man's soul the disciple-

*

One Almighty!
One Great Spirit!
One Life!
One Humanity!
With
One purpose:
To permit life
To unfold in each and every living being!

*

It is man's fondest of blessings
To know that God hears his pleas,
And answers him by quite often not granting
What was petitioned.

*

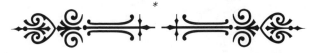

Bless me, my Almighty,
And I shall be blessed.
Heal me, and I shall be healed.
Walk with me, and I shall be strong.
Guide me, and I shall succeed.
Redeem me, and I shall be redeemed.
For You are the life of my life.
You are my All.

*

Your blessings
Blessings are unto you,
And your curses
Curses.

*

Man seeks his own salvation
From the moment of his birth.

*

The ideas of what God is or isn't
Have been handed down to man
Like ragged clothes, moth-eaten and patched.
A man who makes no effort to find out
Who God is and what He means to him
Cannot have peace, nor know truth.

*

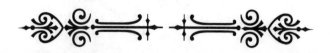

118

As man can recognize his own mind alone,
So in his own mind must he find God.
As man cannot know the mind of another
Except through analogy,
He cannot know God through another man's mind–
Only through his own.

*

To find happiness,
You must have faith,
Faith in life.
This alone will assure your triumph
On the road that you helped mark out for yourself.

*

Belief is not faith.

*

Belief alone
Yields often sorrow,
For disbelief follows
In its footprints.

*

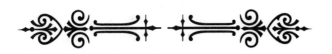

Believe in the unchanging, eternal good
Which is given every man to make his own.
Believe that all conditions within you
Have a reason and purpose.
Believe that your hopes, your prayers
Eventually reach their goal.
Believe that you, in the final end,
Are that goal.

*

No man need believe
In a God,
But each man needs to verify
All Life,
And in time bless his own,
And revere the life of another.

*

Pour not your heart out
To the wind,
For your trouble will not be ended
This way.
Rather believe
The flame of life in your heart
Will show your reason
The way.

*

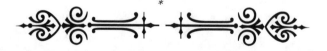

Do not doubt the existence
Of the outer world,
Especially the one that belongs
To your fellow being.

*

Do not use your philosophy or religion
As a whip against anyone,
For darkness so created will await you
In your eternity~

*

Wait not for God to thank you for believing in Him,
Or reward you for what you should do anyway.
If you do,
You are a long way from growing up,
And great shall be your heart's sorrow
When disappointment comes your way.

*

The widest fields of joy,
The mountainous strength of vitality,
Is obtained by him who acquires
Faith in the substance of life.
For such life is the true support
Of all things visible and invisible,
Both within comprehension
And what lies beyond it.

*

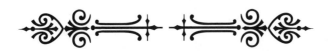

The Shadow of God

When you lack faith,
You admit that you have not the strength
To fight for that which is you.
You are against yourself.
Who, if not you, should take your side?

*

The most vicious person
Is the firmest believer
In the punishment
Of a hereafter hell.

*

He who doubts the Almighty
Will doubt all men.

*

It is not wise to believe
That one is not capable
Of evil.
For until one is strong enough
To withstand evil,
He cannot benefit
From the light of his heart
And receive the radiance that comes to him
In an act of overcoming himself.

*

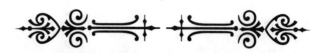

God does not believe.
He works.
*

Believing in anything
Or anyone
Is not knowing
That thing
Or that one.
*

An atheist is as important
In the history of humanity
As the blind believer.
Both contribute to the
Welfare of the whole.
*

People will regard any
Negative evidence as an
Intrusion upon their sacred
Domain of belief,
For the will to believe
Is stronger than common sense.
Lies that support their belief
Will be welcomed without hesitation
And accepted as truths beyond doubt.
*

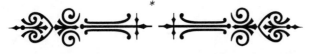

To believe a little is far wiser
Than to believe a lot
And not understand that belief.
*

To believe is not sufficient.
To have faith is not enough.
To know is incomplete.
For in believing, one may acquire doubt.
In faith, one may deny having it.
To know, one may forget.
But to be that belief,
To be that faith,
To be that knowledge,
One is unmoved,
For one is firmly anchored in life,
And life in one.
*

The world is not against any individual.
It is but a certain individual who
Believes that he alone is the world,
And that the world outside of himself is an illusion.
Therefore it does not exist.
Therefore it is not as good as that individual.
Therefore the world becomes unfit to live in.
*

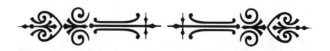

124

The Shadow of God

Each man's beliefs are his mountain.
Upon its summit he may set the course of his day
And view in all directions
The roads to be followed or averted
In the valleys and lowlands of his mind.

*

He who believes in God
May come in time to doubt Him,
But he in whom God believes
Cannot doubt ever.

*

Faith is as inconsistent
As the person professing it.

*

The All Life is unmoved
By man's faith in it
Or by his lack of faith.

*

A faith filled with love for God
Will heal the soul
And the flesh that houses it.

*

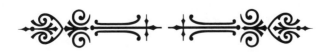

Faith is the substance of imagination,
And hope its wings.

*

Your secret thoughts
Are always made known in time
To God
And to men.

*

Mind, like matter,
Is not supreme.

*

All life is consciousness
Expressed in degrees.

*

Consciousness,
As light,
Has no color
Or dimension.
It is the energy
By which God in man
Is expressed.

*

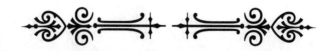

126

Man cannot will
Unity
Within himself,
For the soul does not understand
The will's language
Of force.

*

A master is he who
Captures the perfection
Of the awareness of the moment.

*

Contemplate daily, even for a moment,
The one you love.

*

The words that man
Speaks to himself
May be rumblings
Even to his own ears,
But not to the untiring ears
Of his silent companions
Who walk with him
From the sunrise to the sunset
Of his sleep.

*

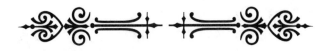

In every home, in every temple,
Near every heart, near everything
That lives and breathes,
A guardian governs the spiritual life.
Be humble, O Man,
That you may well earn what it gives you.
Your debt is not just to those you see around you,
But to those you cannot see
And are nonetheless there.

*

The host of God is no different from you.
When you do good
For someone else's benefit,
At that instant
You are His host,
And He is at your side.

*

Each act is recorded
In the Rock of Ages
Through all time.
The recording angel
Is you.

*

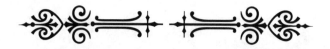

Peace be with you,
My guardian angels,
Ministering angels of the Almighty.
Peaceful be your coming,
Messengers of peace.
Blessed be your stay
With the members of my household.
Share in the wealth of my table
And the joy of our hearts.
May you part in peace
And carry good tidings from our midst.
For you are the angels
Who guard and guide
Our hearts and judgment
By the Most High Almighty.

*

All angels are but man.
They are his mind and heart.
He is them, and they are him.

*

The angel of problems
Keeps man alive;
For through conflict
Man progresses and knows
He is still needed and is alive.

*

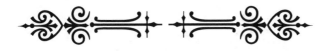

Time is the angel
Who is the chief chemist of living.
He mixes pain and sorrow
With joy and rejoicing,
Defeats with victories,
The known with what is yet to be known.
He alone brings the experience
That makes man human.

*

For the angel of the healing balm
Everyone longs.
He works in our midst
And helps whenever he is called for.
Great is his task, for he heals the many
Though he be but one.
His remedies lie deep in his understanding heart.
He exists in flesh as well as in spirit,
For he carries God Almighty's blessing
In both heart and mind.

*

The character of man
Determines the character of his guardian angel.
Beware, O man,
What you make of yourself!

*

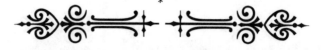

The character of man
Is his guardian angel
Who stands before God,
Representing the man
Even if he finds
No time to commune
With God.

*

An angel, the Tyler,
Keeps watch over your door.
O, how high he points the way!
Yet he keeps man's feet
On the earth firmly fixed.
When the man in his charge
Forces doors to open before their time,
Walks through them into pain,
And, in the end, finds sorrow,
Who awaits with patience?
What angel steers him from peril
Toward a safe, loving path?
O you, who are the high,
Yet are one with man below!

*

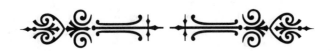

God is always in you.
If you keep Him locked inside,
You will never see or know Him.
Bring Him out of your heart
And place Him before you
That you may see the road
Upon which he leads you.

*

When a person
Seeks the aid of your counsel,
Enter into silence
So your inward judgment
May assist you.
Do not betray your fellow
By rendering only an opinion,
For this he can do for himself.
The counsel he seeks
Must come from your inner heart.
It is a privilege for him to receive it—
And for you to give it.

*

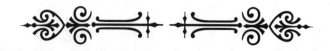

The Shadow of God

Let the Eternal One
Be your partner
Each and every day.
In all your undertakings.
Consult Him first
And heed His counsel.
Then your days will not be lonely,
Your years will be filled with bliss and satisfaction,
Your life will be a success with Him,
And He a success with you.
Do not forget to give Him
His share of the partnership,
For He gave first
Your own self unto you.

*

An unbiased opinion–
Where can it be found?
Even man's gods
Are not free from it.

*

No man can know what is best for another,
Since no man knows what is best for himself.

*

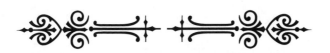

Men have flocked to hear
The words of ill advice
That rend friend from friend,
Wife from husband,
Brother from sister,
Citizen from country~
But the words of
The silent God
Are seldom heeded!

*

He who follows the counsel
Of the foolish
Can never know the counsel of the wise.
He who relies exclusively on the counsel of the wise
Forfeits the right
To think and to live for himself.

*

Everyone on earth is guided
By a spirit~
Be he true or false~

*

Control yourself.
Guide your mind and heart.
But not another's~

*

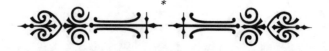

134

Who knows
Whether the arrow
That points toward one's destination
Be true~

*

Treat everyone
As if God were before you
Asking you to help Him.

*

Without the unseen help that each person receives,
He could not exist a single day.

*

Every person has a handicap.
Every individual needs, therefore, another.
Accept this, and know that you are no different
From another
And that your fellow man is like
You, in need of you as you are in need of him.

*

The force that holds mankind together
Is one's need to be helped
And the other's need to help.

*

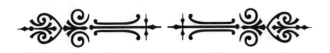

Search for those
Who are in greater need than you,
And you will pleasantly discover
The remedy for your own needs.

*

It is wise to call upon men for help
When only men can do it,
And to call upon God for help
When only God can do it.
God is not where man believes He is.
God is where man finds Him
In each moment of his days.

*

If you are to accept the bread of another,
Fear not to look at him.

*

Build my house for me, O Creator,
That you may dwell with me therein,
And that I may not labor
In vain, should I be required
To build it alone.

*

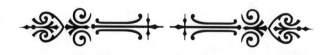

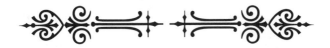

The Shadow of God

The greatest of all charities lies
In treating the one in need of it
With respect,
And esteeming his manhood.
To receive alms is most
Bitter to the one who receives it.
*

The diamond in the mud
Is still a diamond.
So is a man a man
Even in the gutter.
*

The virtue of charity is
Equal in importance to all else—
Mainly, in giving manhood to man.
*

A person may be rich in his youth,
Well provided for in manhood,
But still in the end
He will need the assistance
Of those whom he shunned before.
*

He who is active all his life
Will keep from himself alms' bread.
*

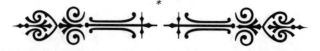

The more the mind and heart are active,
The more one does for another,
The less he will afford to accept charity.

*

It is better to be dependent in youth
Than in hoary years.

*

Bitter is the food on the table
When it is not earned.

*

Man sees youth, manhood, and old age
In one instant.
Therefore he knows his own future.
Let him provide accordingly.

*

All your acts of charity and benevolence
Are the makers of peace
Between you and your fellow~
Between you and your Maker.

*

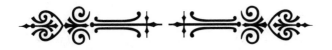

The Shadow of God

If two love each other,
One lives in the love of the other.
If one stumbles and falls,
The other upholds him.
If one dies,
The other remembers him.

*

What may seem unessential to a man
May be a vital necessity for a woman.
Watch therefore how you value
Affairs of the heart.

*

Husband and wife
Stay near each other
Oft because of duty,
Some tradition binding them.
Find the need
For love
To fill the emptiness
Caused by duty.

*

To marry the person you do not love
Is like plowing the world with thorns,
For you shall deal with your children as strangers
And diminish the hope of their life.

*

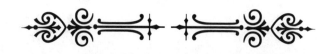

Equal should husband and wife be at home.
None is master over the other.
Let each counsel, love and uphold the other.

*

A man can only open
The door that leads to happiness
When he steps out from behind it
And offers to take someone along.

*

Through human relationships
Is peace maintained
Or war begun.

*

Life is a friend
Who stands by a man's side.
Death is a friend
Who stands by a man's other side.
He who accepts both has nothing to fear,
For life and death are really one and the same-
And are one with the man.

*

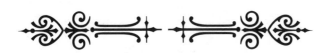

Place yourself
In the center of things.
Never stay about
The fringes—
There is but loneliness there.

*

He who demands friendship
Will find none.
He who begs for it
Will find people running from him.
But he who waits upon many
Will find friendship offered to him.

*

Friends who can be purchased
Will sell out he who bought them
If a competitor offers a higher price.

*

A friend shares what he has
And does not seek its return.
He who seeks return
Reveals that he was not what he pretended to be—
Least of all, a friend.

*

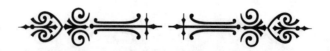

How can he who is a stranger to himself
Hope to find friendship in others?

*

It is better to experience humiliation
Than to suffer the pangs of loneliness.

*

Whether man knows it or not,
He partakes of the companionship
Of God.

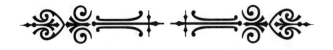

The Shadow of God

ODE TO AMERICA

Weep! Weep!
For us left to mourn those
Wrest from our hearts!

But let us mourn
Not so long
That we keep
Their spirits
Bound to earth
By our love.

At eventide,
As the sweet sun sets,
Let us turn west,
Assembled or alone,
Speaking and singing
For the souls of our dead.

Remember the good
For their country,
Community, and family

They have done!

Let us understand
The difference between
The way of men
With evil intent
Who act through
Destruction and death
And the way of the Almighty,
Who bestows progress

Upon all who live
And will die!

In His hand is the spirit
Of all who live and die.
He alone uplifts our hearts
That we may find peace
In the loving embrace
Of his arms.

Remember always
What the Almighty
Has quickened into life.

It is, was, and shall ever be
His gift to us all,
For we are molded
By the touch of his hand
And his love.

Our souls are meant to be
Like the sun-
Shining, shimmering jewels
Of light on earth
And in the heavens above.

The Almighty watches over His children!
He gives His children work
To do good on earth
For the benefit
Of all the living.
In loving kindness
And with great wisdom
Does he do this.

He raises the souls
Of the dead
And comforts our

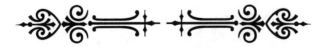

Human hearts.

Let us not, therefore,
Weep for us
Who are left,
Nor mourn for those
Who were from our hearts
By acts of evil
Wrest!

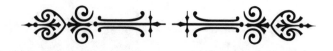

LOVE ABIDES FOREVER

Weep not for me,
Now that I am gone ahead in time!
Shed no tears of grief,
But shed tears of joy,
As I have no more pain
In my body or mind.

As a soul in light,
I am free to grow~
To ascend to the heavens of light
And of beauty
To do what I could not
While I was with you!

You cared for me.
Oh, how you cared for me.
Not just for my body,
But for me-the person
I was and still am!
You gave me your love freely,
Love I could not buy anywhere.

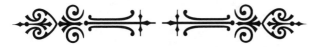

The Shadow of God

149

You nurtured me,
Washed me, fed me, clothed me,
Tutored me, and laughed with me.

When my eyes failed me,
You! You!
Did the seeing for me
That I should not stumble,

That my feet should step
The way they did before.

You held my hands in yours.
You wiped my face.
You touched me with your heart.
Your hands spoke what you felt for me.
Your arms were outstretched
To give me support
When my strength failed me.

Now I will bless you
From where I am
Or will be in God Almighty's time,
For distance does not exist

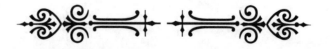

150

Where love abides.

I have been received by angels of light.
In blankets woven in love for me
They wrapped me.
They will carry me to a place
Where I will be happy.

Then will I prepare a place
Where in God's time
I will greet you again,
As I did when I was born on Earth
Under your heart,

And recount the happy times we shared,
Never to depart from one another.
In the glories of God's worlds
We will explore the star-studded heavens,
With angels showing us the way.

But until then,
From time to time
I will come to bring you
Good news, and cheer you up

When you least expect
To talk to your heart.
In the stillness of the night
You will hear me.

And I will tell you
That dying
Is not an end,
But the beginning
Of a journey
That never ends!

152

A PRAYER FOR ARIEL

What the Almighty Yehovah quickened into life,
Behold, it is His gift.
The great Almighty Creator quickened me into life.
Behold, I am the gift of His life!

It is a rose, a flower of sunshine
Molded by the touch of His hand!

I am a rose, a flower of sunshine.

I was and am still being molded by His hand.

To be a living soul, whose light is destined to be
Brighter than a sun!
I am a living soul, destined to be brighter than a sun!

You are the light of my light.
To you I give this Earth and
Her heavens, to be yours forever!
I am the light of His light.
To me He gave the Earth and
Her heavens, to be mine forever.

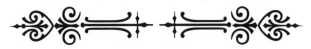

But above all, what I gave to no other animal
On the Earth, or in the waters thereof,
Or in the air of heaven,
Gave I unto you–
Behold, I gave yourself to you!

I behold the greatest gift I ever received–
The gift of myself to myself, to be mine alone!

And I gave you guardian angels to walk by you
And show you my great delights in you
And my unfailing love for you, without end!

And He gave me my guardian angels, who walk by
my side
And bring His love to my soul!

They will speak to your soul
To keep you warm in my love,
To fill your love with my love,
To keep you in the right way!
They speak to my soul, keep me warm in His love,
And keep me in the right way.
But your judgment and self

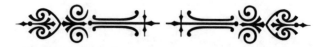

154

I put into your hands alone.
Learn all things through your own judgment
And your soul.
I will learn all things through my judgment and my
soul.

Then spoke Yehovah to the guardian angels—

Into your keeping, my beloved, I give this light,
Ari-el. She is a light of mine, and I bequeath her
unto you. You shall make yourself known to her
spirit, but not to her senses; for the plan of my cre-
ation is for the unending growth and ascent of the
souls of all the living, forever, without end.

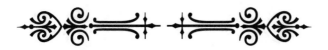

RIBS OF LOVE

As dawn heralds the day, and
Day pursues the evening tide, and
Night the morning light,
So does a man pursue a woman
And a woman a man, eternally.
As life and light are constant companions
In one embrace of one heart and mind in one time,
So should the wisdom of a man be one
With the understanding of a woman
In their two hearts and minds.

A woman was not created out of the head of man,
Nor out of his feet,
As it was decreed that no man ever shall have
The right to rule, to command
Or to walk over her,
Nor shall she be forced
To serve him as a servant,
Nor he her.

She was fashioned equally with him

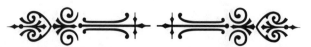

In the mind of God,
"In the image and form"
That dwell in the heart, to be covered forever
By the ribs of love.

She is forever to be free
To choose, to walk with him
Whom she loves, and he
With her, hand and heart
Together, at each other's side,

Protecting one another
From the shadowy phantoms forever
Lurking in the unlit
Moonless and starless nights,

Then
In each other's arms awakening
To the warming rays of their sun of love,
Now rising on the horizon to light their way
On the journey of hope
'Til in the west, in due time,
Their sun will come to rest
To begin anew!

I NEED YOUR SMILE

O friend, do you have a minute's time?
Please, friend, I need your smile.
Stop! and listen? I have a story to tell.
Won't you please listen? Won't you please smile?

There was I, once upon a time,
When someone held me close to their bosom, their
heart,
Someone who cared very much
That I should live and not die.
But now I have none to care.
Won't you please stop and give me at least your
smile?

I ask not for your hand, nor for your wallet.
A nod of your head,
A wave of your hand
Would be enough for me
To know that you care just a little,
Even if you don't smile.
Don't rush by me so fast, O friend.

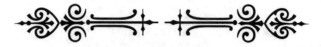

158

Slow down, please, slow down, please.

Take a look, a long look~
My face may be yours,
And your face may be mine!
O friend, all I want is your smile.

Do you now have a minute's time?

No one stops, no one smiles.
A lonesome heart, a lonesome mind.
A burden too heavy to bear.

No one is willing to share a smile.

A wink of the eye is the silent voice of the soul
That brings to pass real hope
That one's life is always there,
Never to abandon you!
It listens, it warms your insides.
It alone is time.

Therefore, friend, rush and rush by me.
Run, run away from me.

I have found my true friend
Who is always with me.
I am not alone, and never was.

My life is Me! And I am with Life!
My life in the All Life has all the minutes of time for
me.

O friend, whoever you are, rushing by me,
Do you now have a minute of time
To listen to me, to hear my story?
No? But I will always be ready to hear you when
you need me!

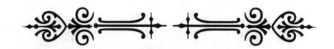

FORGETTULNESS

I woke up today and for a moment
I could not remember my name
Or who I was.
I said to myself, I have arrived
At the threshold of forgetfulness.
Where have my years gone?
I see them not,
Yet they weigh me down.
My back is slightly bent.
My eyes, O, my eyes look to the ground now
Instead of toward the sky.

I know I have lived those years!
But where are they?
Where can I go to review them?
To see what could have been different?
What I have missed?
Would I live them the same
As I did?

I hear a whisper.

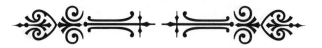

I look here and there, but see no one.
Where are you, inaudible voice?

The answer slowly rises into my consciousness~

I am the sum of your remembrance,
The whisper in your silence, in your dreams
And waking hours.
I am the All, and you alone have made me.
I am All, what you wrote with your hand and heart.

I am the sum of your years,
As you have lived them~
Your smiles, your tears, your joys and your fears,
All your hopes, all your dreams,
Your failures, your successes.
I am your remembrance,
The You that you've become, 'til now!

Tears have carved wrinkles on your face.
In the furrows between your brows
Your worries have been etched.
The lines at the edges of your lips
Are sunshine rays of smiles

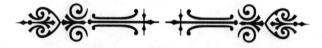

162

And happy times of bygone years.
The glimmer in your eyes still projects
The hopes you have for a future
Yet to be lived, yet to be written by you.

Remember well those thousands of millions
Who had no chance to stand
At the threshold of forgetfulness
And ask, Where have my years gone?

It is these you must not forget!
For they have helped to make you
What you have become.

The voice ceases to speak,
And I sit at the edge of my bed
And think to myself what all this means.
And like a flash, I understand–

Where have the years gone?
They and all the living are I,
I meaning We,
And We and I are One Humanity.

FORGETFULNESS: A REQUIEM

Dedicated to the eleven million,
among them six million Jews,
who perished in World War II
by the evil acts of men.

The requiem of forgetfulness is easily sung,
And forgiveness is readily given
While men's bones hang from trees,
Their ashes in furnaces not yet cool,
Bodies in graves yet unidentified,
The wound of love not yet healed,
The cord of human ties not yet cut,
The shock still so great that no gap is felt
Between those who've departed and those who
remain.
Who will heal all these wounds?
While these things were done,
The sky did not change,
Nor did the Earth move from its orbit.
The sun rose and set.
The stars were seen just the same.

And there is no help for man from any source,
For he retains both his goodness and his evil.
Awake, man—
See what you seek to forget!

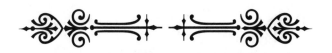

The Shadow of God

From the Furnace of Affliction to the Joy of a New Nation

Not with pearls, gold, silver or diamonds did the Almighty Creator rebuild the Jewish people.

He looked, He searched, He walked by the side roads of every land. Then He halted in Europe, and He saw! He saw the bullet-ridden bodies, the effluvium-scented rags hanging and drenched in the liquefied torsos of children, mothers, fathers, brothers and sisters, uncles and aunts, in unmarked graves, strewn with the ashes formed from bodies taken from furnaces to be mingled in the soil of affliction.

He walked into the camps of death and human abomination. There! There! There! He chose to reclothe the dry, shriveled flesh under the skins left on bony skeletons that could barely stand.

He cried aloud!-and the conscience in man and mankind was stirred. He urged the nations of the earth to allow the children of affliction to return to

that promised land where once dreamt a nation of
His faithful, worshipping and living in peace.

Like their ancestors of ancient past, there they are to
begin their hope, not in any single human being, nor
in any single nation or people, whose inhumanity
may whip them into submission so that their heads
should hang on their chests with eyes searching the
ground beneath their feet for a needless shame~

Nay, but in Him, whose existence humanity has
denied and his own people have forgotten.

Yet He was the silent, living witness to the inhuman~
ness of the nations against them. But because of the
freedom men and nations were granted by Him, they
must assume full responsibility for all those inhu~
mane acts against them.

Children, His children! You are once again chosen
from the furnace of affliction. Join your hearts and
minds with Him, whose eyes are still filled with tears
of sorrow for those whose bodies lie in the bosom of
the earth beneath the starry heavens. They are yet

remembered by those who gave them life and by every decent living human heart!

Build and rebuild that ancient land of promise where every heart is to be bent to improve, to elevate the still grief-stricken souls, so in that land once again should be heard smiling laughter, throats and lips echoing the songs of hope, dancing feet beating out tune after tune. Never again, never again will we permit the beastly nature of men and nations to humble and trample our spirits to feed the furnaces of affliction with the living bodies of our old and young!

168

CONTEMPLATION

Rivers of blood have cut deep gorges
In the surface of the earth.
No farmer has grown a kernel of corn
In a patch of land
That was not fertilized by human blood.
There was not a soldier who prayed to his God
That his enemy be spared
And his own life be taken in his place.
Nay-prayers of thankfulness on lips
Were offered for victories won
While the ears of the dying
Still heard.

GRATITUDE

Where once teepees stood,
Where the bronze man loved his woman,
Now stands triumphant
The monument of forgetfulness.
In tearless eyes,
Through eternal nights,
He gazes from the past
Upon us all
And wonders who will remember,
Who will say
Thank you, O Brother,
For sharing with us
This land~

SILENT EARTH

The Earth is silent.
She cannot speak.
We curse her,
Yet she does not care.
We dread her
In our foolish fear.
We run away from her-run-
Run-but where?
Only to her.

She is cold,
Yet warm in heart.
She covers the tears
We shed in our nights,
Yet we cannot see
That out of her heart
Issues the peaceful sea,
And that in her veins
Flow the streams
Of the silvery night,
And her nerves pulsate

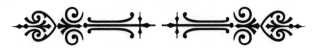

The golden days
Of our faith.

No-we cannot see
That her hair
Is the wheat
Of our golden fields,
And that her hands
Are the crust of our bread.
No-we cannot see

Her breast to be
The grapes of our wine,
And her eyes to be
The luminous stars.

We are afraid.
We say that she drinks
Our blood.
We abuse her-
Bring her to shame-
We shout!
Out loud!
"O Earth! Thou harlot,

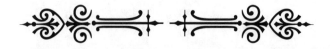

Thy passions
The vulcans of destruction;
Thy love,
Quicksand of devastation;
O Earth,
Canst thou not see
Why we fear thee?"

No~
Do not say
That we must go
And leave you behind~
No~
Not 'til my soul
Has beheld thy beauty
In the light
That you, my love, my life, are~
Mother of my birth,
You are the silent Earth.

FACES

How sweet to behold
The face of a new birth,
The innocence of that hallowed
First light and life,
Bringing new hope
From its source, the Almighty,
To the family of humanity;
This new birth a blessing, not a curse,
To all who live upon this
Our Mother Earth.

The wind of time moves swiftly upon
The new birth,
Shaping and molding it into
The now smiling
And then crying face
As it responds to the love
Or hate it receives from its mother,
Father, brother, sister,
Friend or foe
In the cradle

From the human family.

That face-O that sweet face!
If it is fortunate to have reached
Youthful years-
Now, humanity's future hope!
Not yet cut down by
Drugs, discord, guns in the streets,
War and famine;
Its fragile, expanding mind

Not turned against the law and order
Of civilized society
Or against itself,
Seeking to end its own life
For some foolish, unworthy cause.
It may now have a chance to reveal
Its spirit's exuberance,
Its zest for life, happiness,
The love and passion growing
In its heart and mind.

Now the rushing waves of the wind
Of mortal time

Readies that face
To assume the political maturity
Of the adult,
Expressed as follows:
The one he shows,
The one he hides,
The one he sees
In the mirror of the eye
In the face of another,
The one that is true
But that he seldom sees—
Yet which remains
Revealed before God
And his own life
And his own soul.

All these faces! Rolled into one!
Now molded, now seen
In the face of an aged one,
Where acceptance of self
Becomes an opportunity—

As well as its rejection.
Its soul's mantle forms from regrets

Solidly so woven.
To those faces, forgiveness is yet to be given
And by the soul gracefully received.

Alas! The end of the journey
Of that new face of birth
Is now signaled,
Its hallowed first light and life
Replaced with written testimony
Etched in wrinkles and
Furrowed around the eyes,
Attesting to a time lived
And lessons learned or cast aside.

These times are never again to be relived
Here! Here on this
Our Mother Earth!
The light of the new birth
Now gone out of the mortal face
Puts on the face of its eternal soul
And begins to shine in far-off worlds
Unencumbered by mortal fears.

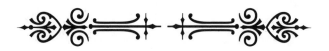

The Shadow of God

IN THE EVER PRESENT MOMENT

Somewhere, some place,
The sun is shining,
Storms raging,
Rivers flooding,
And gentle rain
The ground is touching.
Somewhere, some place
In the ever present moment,
Fires are sizzling,
Burning crops, forests or homes–
And in many homes,
Bodies are warming.

Somewhere
In the ever present moment,
Winds are blowing
In the leaves,
Gently rustling;
In the mountains, shrilling;
And over the oceans, roaring,
Speaking the silent name

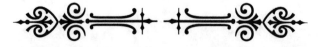

The Shadow of God

Of the ever present moment.

In the ever present moment,
Somewhere, some place,
Lions are roaring or napping,
Hyenas with dingoes, jackals and vultures
For prey competing,
Wolves in forests howling,
While cows, goats and camels
With their milk the hungry feeding,

Lambs and vicunas their wool
To man donating.
Somewhere in the ever present moment
The horse and the ass
Are man's burdens sharing
Dogs their love freely giving,
And serpents for rodents foraging.
Somewhere, some place
In the ever present moment,
All earthly beasts–
The fowl of heaven, the fish in rivers,
And denizens of the oceans and seas–
Are their lives to mankind offering,

Their blessings giving.

Somewhere in the ever present moment
Children are being born and dying.
Somewhere, some place,
Children are dancing
And from hunger starving.
Monstrous men
Their ears, noses, feet and hands
Are maiming.
Somewhere
In the ever present moment
Children are learning.
Someplace
Children are in slavery working.
Somewhere, some place
In the ever present moment,
Fetuses are aborting.
Somewhere, some place,
Children are abandoned

While other children
Love are embracing.

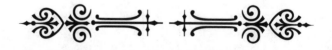

180

Somewhere,
In some place
In the ever present moment,
The sun is setting,
The moon rising,
The stars shining.

Somewhere
At this moment
Young hearts are embracing,
And somewhere two hearts
Are separating.
Somewhere
At this moment
Someone is mourning,
Young men and women
In uniform their country guarding,
And somewhere these young ones
In battlefields with their bodies decorating,
And mothers, fathers, widows, and orphans
Are crying.
Somewhere, someplace,
Tyrants are sitting and planning,
To the world chaos bringing,

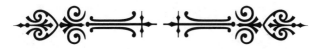

The Shadow of God

While others are rising,
Peace heralding.

Somewhere, some place
In the ever present moment,
Men and women
The fields are cultivating

With shovels, hoes and plows
The ground turning,
And butter churning.
Somewhere
At this moment
Men and women are in comfort sleeping
And others in doorways and gutters
Are dreaming.
Somewhere at this moment
Some are embracing
While others in anger
With fists are slapping,
With knives cutting,
With guns wounding and killing.

Somewhere in this ever present moment

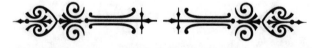

182

Hope is rising,
The heart and mind warming.
Somewhere
At this moment
Justice is at the helm
And somewhere, some place, justice is lacking.
Somewhere, some place,
In hearts, love is rising
And goodness in hearts dwelling.
Somewhere in the ever present moment
A good day on the horizon is dawning
With a promise of a future
Filled with good tidings,
Brightly shining.
Somewhere, some place
In the ever present moment,
Young and old, hand in hand,
Hearts are warming,

Children in schools learning,
And slavery's chains very slowly falling,
Freedom's sun now beckoning,
The bells of joy ringing,
Making faces smiling.

183

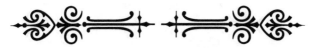

The Shadow of God

Awake, awake!
Better days all must create
Day by day,
Night after night.
Each other in love embrace
Somewhere in the ever present moment.
Let us accept
The Almighty's love,
For each lives in the moment,
And He is the ever present moment.

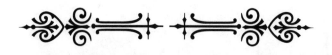

The Circle

That which was without beginning
Or without end
Contains all within it.
Each and every living being is an end
Of a ray of life and light
Focused in mortality.
All things impress upon him
From the Great External.
Man is but a center,
Not the circumference.

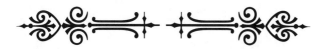

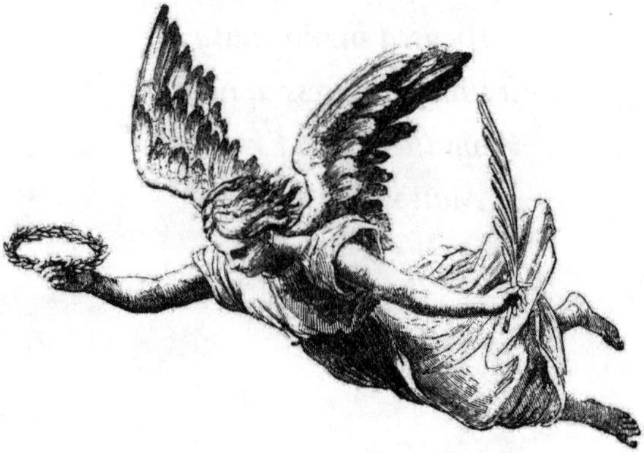